Open Heart Chronicles

Open Heart Chronicles

Poems by James B. Moore

edited by
Phil Bevis

CHATWIN BOOKS
SEATTLE, 2019

Open Heart Chronicles by James B. Moore

Poems and afterword copyright the author.
Edited by Phil Bevis. Cover design by Annie Brulé.
Cover artwork by Dean Kelly.
Book design by Phil Bevis, Annie Brulé and Cyra Jane Hobson.
Editorial and design content copyright Chatwin Books, 2019.
All rights reserved. Set in Garamond and Pabst typefaces.

Visit us on the web at www.ChatwinBooks.com

ISBN paperback: 978-1-63398-094-5

ISBN hardcover: 978-1-63398-095-2

to Esther

*you are the one
through whom love
and this book flows*

contents

poems

nine lives

I'm like an alley cat
who has lived most of his
nine lives

there's freedom
in knowing the
end is near

life feels more real
when any moment
might be my last

I don't fear
what awaits
or what comes next

curiosity does not kill this cat
I can smell
the scent of something more

men in my family

when I was ten I
worked at the newsstand after school
it felt good to make money

Chicago's south side in the 50's
was a tough hard place
I got mugged twice

kept working
dad said nothing and
I never got robbed again

years after his death
mom shared with me
that he had kept watch

out of sight
to keep me safe
insisting she not tell

men in my family
didn't talk much
they just showed up

kenny

going to school in
South Chicago in the 50's
meant learning to fight

you stood up for yourself
or you'd get
pushed around

my best friend Kenny
wouldn't fight
just walked away

he was kind
but didn't show emotions
I never saw him angry

Kenny's father drank
and beat him
so we played at my place

when my family moved
I missed my
quiet loyal friend

years later it shocked me
to learn he had
gone to prison for murder

some guy paid the price
for everyone who ever
pushed Kenny around

the one kid
in our school
who turned the other cheek

ended up
locked away
for the public good

alienation
(to E. F. Norwood, 1927-2016)

my high school debate coach
demeans a
girl on the team
I call him on it

he sneers "if you don't
like it you can leave"
so I do
the entire team walks with me

this made me unpopular
with other teachers
I developed an attitude
a silent "don't tread on me"

my English teacher
had a reserve of his own
returned my silence
right back at me

the books we read
were filled with
powerful voices
capturing my imagination

Mr. Norwood sentenced each of
us to a different novel
mine was
Crime and Punishment

it felt like
doing hard time
but page by page
my perspective shifted

with each chapter
I was sobered
by the consuming power
of alienation unleashed

in later years we became close
sharing drinks and laughter
what started with resentment
evolved into friendship

unloading

one summer fresh out of
high school I worked for the
Seattle Post Office
unloading mail

three of us
would empty freight cars
throwing 50 pound mail sacks
onto carts

it didn't pay much
and there wasn't
always enough
work

so we rotated, two unloading
while the third napped
behind stacks of sacks
in the freight car

one day we forgot about
the third guy napping
he woke up
in Canada

he was fired
but got a job up the line
loading those same cars
with those same damn bags

back at us
two nap-deprived
short handed
wise-assed kids

a manly man

working as a seaman in
Alaska I met a young guy who
worked on John Wayne's yacht

over drinks he shared
a story about the
manly actor and his wife
a fiery Latin beauty

late one night
he heard
drunken yelling and
the sound of breaking dishes

Wayne staggered to the deck
head bleeding
tears in his eyes mumbling
"I just don't understand women"

in that moment I
never liked John Wayne
more

all drummed out

I once dated an
Ice Capades skater who
described the forty-year old
drummer in the band
as the only straight
male on the tour

he spent his nights
comforting the
girls in the show who
would get lonely
as they moved from
town to town

he had an ashen pallor
and seemed exhausted
looking years older than his age
it appeared that what some men
would regard as paradise
was killing him

join the army and see the world

joining the Army reserve
to avoid Vietnam
I leave basic training
for three months as a clerk

the Army assigns me to a
unit that deploys soldiers
to Korea and
to Vietnam

I quickly see
they're taking bribes
shipping guys to Korea
to dodge Vietnam

the sergeant in charge
is a tough mafia type
and definitely not happy
I'm there

catching him alone I say
"bet you don't want me around"
he glares at me
says "you're right"

I offer to keep my mouth shut
in exchange for him letting me
disappear
with a long hard look he agrees

I rent a room in town
at night play music in a bar
by day hang out with
new friends on the beach

I find
new meaning to
"join the army
and see the world"

in the john with bob

two army reservists
avoiding the Vietnam draft
meet in basic training

after lights out
we talked in the head
of literature, philosophy, girls, future plans

Bob knew he wanted to write novels
music had almost killed me so
I didn't know what to do next

he talked me into
joining him
to go back to college

looking back I wonder how many other
soldiers found their path
talking in the john

back in the world

returning to college
I arrive in Ellensburg in winter
walk out of the Greyhound bus station
into the Antlers Hotel

carrying my guitar and duffle bag
step into the hotel bar
needing a little courage before
making my way to the dorm

a few drinks help me talk
to the friendly bartender
tell her about leaving music and drugs
planning to get a degree

she gives me directions
to the campus dorm
I stagger out into the cold
wanting to walk off the drinks

damn cold freezing cold
walking longer than I realize
slipping on snow and ice
I find myself in the stockyards, lost

shivering, I stumble
my way back to the hotel
sit down at the same bar
where I'd started

seeing me too chilled to talk
the bartender buys me
a few more drinks
then offers to drive me to the dorm

carries my bag
helps me through the door
kissing me on the cheek
she leaves

standing in a small room
greeted by three wide-eyed freshman
I've just landed
back in the world of children

begin again

back to college
afraid my mind might be
too damaged to learn

succeeding this time
means quitting drugs
harder than I thought

trying to study
lightning flashes of pain
rip through my head

reading becomes so hard
I crash backwards in
my chair

hit the floor
pick myself up
reset the chair

pushing through the fog
of dead brain cells I begin
the one future left

education

after the first term I
rent a house near campus
a more adult environment

younger English profs would
drop by to discuss edgy
literature not in the curriculum

we all share our writing
I was transitioning from
social protest rock lyrics to poetry

one afternoon I share a poem with
a teacher and poet
he listens, sips a beer, puffs his pipe

says "I like your poem, man, but you
might want to sound less like you're
standing on the coffee table shouting"

for the first time
I was glad I returned
my real education had begun

spyder

winter quarter
Ellensburg is freezing
and buried in snow
I walk past a pet shop

spot a tiny black puppy
runt of the litter
shivering alone in the window

looking so lost and hopeless
I rescue him
stuff the hairball under my coat
carry him home

half chihuahua half miniature poodle
he's like an angora rat
so ugly he's beautiful
I name him Spyder

encourage him to
play the Pied Piper
fetching girls
leading them my way

after graduation he becomes
lonely waiting daily for me to
return from teaching so sadly
I give him to my parents

my father tells me about
the girls who circle around him as
he walks Spyder on the beach
Spyder's web still works

point made

leaving college
beginning teaching
I bring my little
Spyder dog with me

rent a house with
a teacher who
avoiding Spyder makes it clear
he dislikes dogs

one morning my dog is limping
his hind leg hurting
I ask my housemate
if he kicked him

the man looks nervous
denies it weakly
I tell him never
touch my dog again

returning home from teaching
the guy finds
a small brown pile on his pillow
when he complains I smile
thinking Spyder's a dog after my own heart

the designated drunk

driving over steep
mountain passes
on a dark curvy road
from Yakima to Ellensburg
with three friends passed out

the designated drunk
I drive
contrive a game
to stay awake
twenty-five miles
without touching the brakes

totally focused
up over
around the hills
a heightened sense
of being

tires screaming
through the curves
a greater challenge
than I guessed

finally
feel relief
to see
the lights
of Ellensburg

the road levels out
easing up on the gas
car slowing down
I touch my foot
to the brakes

the pedal slams
flat to the floor
no brakes
there are
no brakes

downshifting
pull the emergency
jerking us all
to a stop

my friends awaken
hear me
mumbling
about the game
without any brakes

was it just a game
that was a way
to get us
all home alive

or was there
something more
that kept us
on the road

journey

I have been protected
during times of peril
in many humbling
ways

have been held by light
by the love I found
when I drowned
and was sent back

spirit has kept a failing heart
functioning
helped me speak
with the dead

led me back
to a beloved
soulmate
kept me from harm

sometimes others get
uncomfortable when I
address the spirit
that surrounds us

embracing us with
an energy
that cannot be
fully known or spoken

when I share
experiencing other presences
during my day I've
learned to be selective
about who I tell

each of us is on
a journey
interpreting it
our own way

suspended in air

speeding
through the mountains
careening toward my
wedding

my sports car's first trip
best man beside me
new roads ahead
a light wind at our backs

we're driving full out
taking sharp turns
exhilarated
by the rush

the car loses traction
slides to the outside of
the curve
two wheels suspended in air

it feels like slow motion
I hold fast to the wheel
knowing that's all
I can do

a gust of wind
surges up from the void
under the car's
hanging edge

we land back on the road
four wheels on the ground
away from the
brink of the cliff

the car is still moving
no place to pull over
just keeping my wits
slowing down

we drive on in numb wonder
suspended in silence
awed by the
force of the wind

neighbors

during the late '60s
looking for cheap rent
my wife and I move
into a run-down neighborhood

we rent a funky house
park our old sports car
on the street in front
where we can watch it

our mostly unemployed neighbors
welcome us
share fresh vegetables
from their gardens

across the street a neighbor
with a large white van
peppered with bullet holes
motions me over

says "you don't know this
but we all keep
watch over your car"

"it's easier for me
if you use my garage
hell
I don't use it, anyway"

fancy houses don't make
good neighborhoods but
good neighbors do

house sitting

moving into our
new house my
wife and I find it
occupied

we hear the sounds
of chains rattling in
the attic
locked dutch doors
wide open in the morning

a woman's voice moans
cries out in pain
we talk to the ghost
ask it to
accept us

life returns to normal
over years we forget
stop thinking about the
haunting

going on vacation
we invite a friend
to house sit
returning we find him
upset, circles under his eyes

waving his arms and talking fast
he describes rattling chains
moaning
closed doors
opening themselves

"don't ever ask me
 to house sit again" he whispers
 uncorking a bottle of wine
 we explain our invisible housemate
 our friend drinks
 but does not promise to return

a world of not

we live in a world of not
one is judged
by what is not
rather than what is

the nots fall equally on
everyone
each judges the other by
what is not familiar

when sharing my story
a neighbor replies
"I can't imagine how
that could be"

observing his quickness to
deny my experience
I disentangle from
his not

moving to another country

my wife and I
talk about moving
to another country

I tell her I think I'd
get lonely living in
a different culture

I need people of
my own kind that
I can disapprove of

offerings

I'd rather write
for myself and have
no public
than write for others
and have no self

If I share with others
what I have to offer
and they are uninterested
then I have nothing to offer them

I'm not sure if it is
age or wisdom that
leaves me comfortable with
that thought

on my knees

it's a sunny day
under a clear sky
I visit my father's grave
two years after
his death

taking care of family
meant stuffing my feelings
but I can contain them
no longer

on my knees
sobbing
part in anger part in sadness
at my father's suicide

I tell him
of my guilt
about keeping my distance
all those years

I ask him for
help, for forgiveness
for some way
to carry on

through the fog of
tears it seems like
some part of him
appears above his grave

his shadowy presence gives me strength
and then moves on
allowing me
to do the same

an armload of regret

one day in the last stage of
a failing marriage I visit a
local flower shop

and buy my wife's favorite
roses knowing like everything
else it won't be enough

a pretty young girl working there
smiles at me
in a familiar way

flirts with me
then tells me I dated her mom
"I remember you made her happy"

"I'm 18 now
I want you to
make me happy too"

my mind floods
I grab the roses
rush out of the shop

I went in to get flowers
and left with
an armload of regret

go figure

some women got
angry with me
because
I didn't want to
spend my life
with them

and some got angry
because
I did

epitaph

once again I've
lost my way
I could whine about it
or simply move on

embracing the lesser
of the evils I smile
and imagine my epitaph
which will read

"considering the
whirlpool he
was swimming in
he did well"

nocturnal dilemma

decades of struggle
battling the night

alone in the dark
wrestling with sleep

drowning in shadows
gasping for breath

dreading the void
pushing back death

fear losing my body
life's dreams incomplete

eternally trapped
in surrender or fight

the honeymoon house

my realtor
shows me a
cozy house
an estate sale

walking in
I feel a
real warmth as
I look around

the agent
describes a couple who
moved in on their
wedding day

he passed away last year
she stayed until she
died three months ago
called it her honeymoon house

after buying it and moving in
I would sense
her playful
presence

working in my office
I would find
she had hidden
my stamps

a woman friend
walking through the house
late at night
gives a startled sound

says she saw a
luminous female presence
standing there
not ready to leave

but after I painted the walls
she disappeared
maybe nothing familiar
left to cling to

musing
I think how interesting
how little it took
to help her on her way

observing

there are so many ways to
paint a bird
so many possible intentions

Richard Kirsten Diansai once painted
a playful jibe at his rival Morris Graves
in response to Graves' *Bird And Insect*

Diansai titled his painting
Watching Bird and Insect
like Graves' bird
at first it looked simple

but above the bird
blended with clouds and mist
spirits watch

an architect I know
compared that bird with
a crow, also painted by Daiensai

he told me the crow
looked more real
and was a better representation

seeing only line and structure
he missed the watching spirits
which for me
was the essence of the painting

daiensai

my friend, a
Zen priest and artist
died the way he lived

awakening from a coma
in his hospice bed
as his nurse was giving him
a sponge bath

he told her
"you're beautiful, thank you"
and quietly drifted away

those last words of
truth and gratitude
are both his essence and
his epitaph

browsing

if you try to visit Red's
L.A. bookstore to browse his
signed first editions you'd
be asked to leave

I tell my lady friend
about Red's rule
she smiles and says "don't
worry just leave it to me"

the day we visit Red she
wears a low cut V-neck
sweater with no bra
leans over the counter in that certain way

Red takes the hook
grins like a hashish addict
engages in serious conversation
with her breasts

he lets me take my time
exploring Bukowski books at will
from that day on Red becomes
my newest and best L.A. friend

unshattered cool

Mose Allison plays at a
small Seattle jazz club
sings funky songs
to an enthusiastic crowd

he and his quartet
play in front of a large window
they're in a groove when
the bouncer tosses a drunk out the door

from outside the drunk
heaves a brick through the window
showering glass
all over the performers

the band
dives off the stage
leaving Mose not missing
a beat

he finishes his song like
he's done a hundred times before
it takes more than broken glass
to shatter that man's cool

in my life

in my life I have
learned there are
three things I can
control

who I hang out with
how I react
and whether I listen
to my heart

i saw you

I saw you
you were kind
sincere beautiful
I felt love at first sight

still it was a long wait
the fruit needed to
ripen on the vine
until you re-emerged

my heart opened
I hoped so deeply
you would feel
the way I did

I saw you then
I see you now
I want to see you
forever

why you

the first part
of my life
I was half broken
incomplete

I spent my time
with women who
were just like me
in their own ways

what I found in you
was not a fix
to my brokenness
or the answer to all my needs

I found
kindness and friendship
someone to laugh with me
who believed in me

someone to share the moment
merge our dreams
no one who sees me with you
questions why I love you

they celebrate
how we blend
the way we smile
that I have found you

trying to explain

have you ever
been so devastated
it felt like

being caught in a sandstorm
stripped of your skin
moment by moment

that is how I
would feel if I ever
lost your love

phoenix rising

my wife and I hike
Mount Baker climbing
a high winding trail

I'm suddenly drawn
from the trail
up a steepened rockslide

instinctively know
something is
calling me

find a gray sculpted
rock shaped like
an ancient axe head

the bottom half of one
side partially coated with
golden sandstone

the likeness
of a phoenix bird
rises up from the ashes

past its eyes
a streak of light moves
into golden sun

from yet another angle
I see a regal face
merging with the phoenix

I find deeper insight
into the transformations
of my ever changing life

nature's art has given me
a message
filling me with a quiet wonder

rising from the
ashes of my many former lives
I am the phoenix

with a caring partner
a new home
renewed passion for my life

an extra sensory message
I am truly not alone
one life ends another one begins

endings and beginnings
blend into golden glow
loss becomes rebirth
I arise
but not alone

the mix

mixing cream and sugar
into dark strong coffee
I stir a whirling circle

I am an alchemist
mixing bitter and sweet
sadness and joy

life is the drink and
when stirred
has flavor greater than its parts

last chance

walking from our condo
to the beach
in Playa del Carmen
has its drawbacks

the main street is
lined on both sides
by vendors
and hawkers

we can't get there
without passing
through this avenue
of harassment

over time
I become irritated
with them not taking no
for an answer

one vendor
makes me smile
calls me
Meester Wheeskers

the last day
he shouts
"Hey Meester Wheeskers
last chance
to get screwed"

yucatan cenote

stepping down ancient stone stairs
we descend into a limestone cave
joining others
we strip down to swimsuits
enter a circular seemingly bottomless
pool, a cenote

light a hundred feet up
streams down through a
hole in the ceiling
large vines dangle from
the teeming jungle above

those reluctant to swim
dangle their feet in the dark water
cling to edges
look up in wonder

my wife and I swim to
the center float on our backs
lose all sense of time and space
drawn into this temple of light

the vines move
beckon us to join the dream
to suspend our thoughts
to be

pulled up into air
I find
the world has
disappeared

lost in the moment I am
immersed in a vision the
ancients must have known before
becoming one
with the all

the crystal skull

visiting Carmel California
reliving old memories
I enter a unique
antique shop

spot two crystal skulls
one cracked and flawed
the other perfect and clear
ask the owner to hand me the clear one

acting frightened and shaken he
asks me to remove it from its
container will not touch it
offers to reduce the enormous price by half

says he bought it from a Chinese collector
who discovered the skull in Nepal
the former property of monks
claims it is hundreds of years old

holding the skull fiery waves
pulse through my mind
a band of steel tightens around
my brain

the band grows tighter
there is a roaring sound
I fear my mind could be lost
enveloped in darkness never to emerge

barely able to
place it back in the box
I say goodbye
stagger out the door

I don't know what that energy
was or where it came from
only that there are some things in
this world that are too dark for me

running water

ten of us meet
in a sacred space on Halloween
the night when the veil is thinnest

a shaman teaches
how to communicate
with the dead

we practice
calling forth
the spirits of our families

make offerings of
food and drink
to welcome a visit

hear the sound
of running water
despite no water
on the land

separating
we move into forest
concentrate
on calling those we've lost

I call my
grandfather
who died
when I was ten

he appears
looking drawn and weary
says "prepare
for your death"

not what I
expected
but it certainly
got my attention

stopped at the door

I return home
having spent time
with a shaman
learning how to
commune with
the dead

my wife
stops me at the door
energetically brushes me off
saying "it looks like
you've picked up
a hitchhiker"

three o'clock in the morning

always two knocks
never anyone there
mostly only I hear it

a few times
my wife has
heard it too

maybe someone or something
from the other side
is letting me know
I am not alone

stumbling

walking with
my publisher to
his production studio
I stumble

he helps
me up
with concern asks
are you OK?

brushing it off I say
I'm fine
but getting older
is a trip

at the studio
he seems in a hurry
to complete
my new book of poems

half kidding I ask
are you rushing
to finish it before
I die?

I get no answer but
a wry smile
he
returns to the poems

banking

one day at eighty-seven
after a lifetime of independence
my mom asks me for help

it seems like a small task
to drive her to the bank
and convert an investment

surprised at her request I know this
is a dramatic shift from
the past

inside the bank she
struggles to understand
loses her concentration

seeing her falter
the banker grows kinder
simplifies the explanation

grateful for the banker's kindness
I sadly begin to support
my mother in her decline

now fifteen years later mom is gone
I'm in my seventies
feeling more dependent

increasingly grateful
banking
on the kindness of others

try again

during a colonoscopy
I go into
rapid heartbeat
almost flatline

they stop
try again
once again I
almost flatline

with the courage
of the well sedated
I say "I feel lucky,
let's try again"

the doctor says "no
if we had to crack you open
mopping your blood off the floor
would be a real drag"

surgery

two stents
open clogged arteries
save my
life

afterward
my surgeon says
"you'll need
a burn"

I'm awake on the table
to report the pain
as surgeons work up
through my artery

they burn parts of
my heart
while I chat
with the nurses

thinking of anything
but the operation
I sell them my
book of poems

after the procedure
the surgeon has bad news
they can offer only radical surgery but
other organs might become damaged

I describe my father
dying one organ
at a time
"I'd rather kill myself"

he supports my position
offers an experimental drug
to slow my heart from racing
to live the life that's left for me

someone

lying in a hospital bed
alone
in a single room
the door shut
calling out
trying not to move

determined
fingers applying pressure
on a bleeding artery in
my groin
waiting
listening

I've dropped the call button
can't reach it
without releasing
the spurting
streaming
blood flow

shouting
again and again
no one comes
we thought the worst
was over
my recovery assured

but the blood is pulsing
hand on groin
pressing hard
I wait for someone
to help

side effects

I ask
my doctor
about side effects
of his prescribed heart medication

"the side effect is
life" he tells me
"you need it to
stay alive"

I tell him I'm
concerned that some people
who take it get
dementia

"It's a small percentage" he
assures me
then says "besides
you'd probably never know"

zen revisited

as I age I
remember the zen saying
"chop wood
carry water"
change it to
take pills
make water

cardiac rehab

at cardiac rehabilitation
while working out I
discuss my healing process
with a nurse

I mention our pro football team
known for turning around
a losing game
in the fourth quarter

she smiles and says
"you're not in the fourth quarter,
Jim.
for you it's overtime"

impermanent

everything is
impermanent
that's both the
challenge
and the
delight
of it all

uncorked

there's a
difference
between living
and existing

the same wine that brings
life to my days
disagrees with the medication
that keeps my heart alive

I try to find
that tricky balance
between feeling alive
and being alive

I may drink less wine
than I like
but at least I can say
the bottle of my life is
open not corked

a broader sense of love

once it was about women
then about career
now a broader spectrum

I have new songs to sing
new poems to write
a broader sense of love

the simplest sights
offer new perspective
new ways to be

in morning light
I hear enveloping spirit
calling me

to what we
were born to
remember

always

in the light of
each morning
I watch you rise

I find love
at first sight
again and again

this will happen
as long as
I live

you've been my
love at first light
love at first sight
day after day
for decades now

and as long as
I breathe
you always will

life

life is a tiny
one-act play
that needs rewriting

a light filled moment
brings awareness
in the theater of my mind

as my performance
on this stage
nears its end

the only audience
that matters to me
is you, my love
is you

the one thing

the one thing in life
that makes me happiest
isn't small in my eyes
though it might be in others'

no one could ever know
the joy and wonder
that fills my heart
when I see you smile

knowing

I have come back
from death
returned from the light
back through the veil

if you have been there
you know
if you have not
perhaps you will

doctors tell me
my heart could stop at any time
I don't worry about dying
my attention, my intention is on life

life here
life now
life with
the one I love

remembering

I don't look forward
to pain
but I don't fear death

the essence of being
is that we are born
of oneness

having passed over
and been called back
I always miss that light
that love

I cherish this life
but always long
to cross back

staying

I have yearned
to return to
the other side
but prefer to
enjoy the wonder
of my life
with you

there will be
ample time
for
what comes next

afterword

Open Heart Chronicles as a title is reflective of several some-what intertwined threads in my life.

The first is fairly literal, in that I have had some serious issues with my heart, and a series of cardiac procedures which result-ed in near death on more than one occasion. These followed an episode earlier in life where I was resuscitated after nearly drowning. What I experienced then was an overwhelming sense of light and love, so welcoming and powerful that it was difficult to come back.

That I have physically survived these challenges is due to the skills and kindness of others. My thanks for the gentle care I have received from many in the medical field is beyond the ability of words to express.

The second is that, when I look back over the years, there have been many occasions when my life was on the edge, and I was saved by someone, or something. I could not have survived alone, and I have the very real sense that I in fact did not.

Third is an increasing awareness, as I near the end of my time in this physical realm of existence, that my experience after death, shared by so many others, is merely the smallest part of something wondrous that is to come.

While part of me deeply yearns to return to that place of light, I am grounded in this life by the love and companionship I share with my soulmate. She makes every morning a joy, every day a dance of belonging, and gives every night a sense of true peace and tenderness.

So I live in the moment, thankful for every day in this world, and for the beauty, friendship, love, and learning that every day can bring.

—*Jim Moore, October 2018*

index of poems by title